My Heart Soars

hancock
house

by Chief Dan George
and Helmut Hirnschall

HANCOCK HOUSE PUBLISHERS

ISBN 0-919654-15-0

Library of Congress Catalog
Card Number 74-78350

Designed by Nicholas Newbeck Design.
Type set in Palatino by White Computer Typesetting.
Printed in Canada.

This book was originally prepared and
published in Canada in 1974 by

Hancock House Publishers, Ltd.
3215 Island View Road, Saanichton, British Columbia, Canada.

This book is simultaneously published in Canada,
for distribution only in Canada from Saskatchewan east, by

Clarke, Irwin and Company Ltd.
Clarwin House, 791 St. Clair Ave. W. Toronto.

ISBN 7720-0743-8

 HANCOCK HOUSE PUBLISHERS, LTD.

My People's Memory
Reaches into the
Beginning of All Things.

Chief Dan George

THANKS:

TO MY FATHER!

For he gave me skill, stamina
and the knowledge of my past.

TO MY MOTHER!

For she gave me the love for life
and taught me to respect it.

TO MY WIFE!

Because she shared my burden
when it threatened to slow my
pace and kept by my side when
we travelled lightly.

TO MY CHILDREN
AND THEIR CHILDREN!

Because in their eyes
I have seen myself.

THIS IS GOOD!

My mother had a kindness
that embraced all life.
She knew her place well
and was comfortable in giving
everything she had.

This is the tradition
of native women.

Young people
are the pioneers
of new ways.
Since they face
too many temptations
it will not be easy
to know what is best.

Words to a Grandchild

Perhaps there will be a day
you will want to sit by my side
asking for counsel.
I hope I will be there
but you see
I am growing old.
There is no promise
that life will
live up to our hopes
especially to the hopes of the aged.
So I write of what I know
and some day our hearts
will meet in these words,
—if you let it happen.

In the midst of a land
without silence
you have to make a place for yourself.
Those who have worn out
their shoes many times
know where to step.
It is not their shoes
you can wear
only their footsteps
you may follow,
—if you let it happen.

You come from a shy race.
Ours are the silent ways.
We have always done all things
in a gentle manner,
so much as the brook
that avoids the solid rock
in its search for the sea
and meets the deer in passing.
You too must follow the path
of your own race.
It is steady and deep,
reliable and lasting.
It is you,
—if you let it happen.

You are a person of little,
but it is better to have little
of what is good,
than to possess much
of what is not good.
This your heart will know,
—if you let it happen.

Heed the days
when the rain flows freely,
in their greyness
lies the seed of much thought.
The sky hangs low
and paints new colors
on the earth.

After the rain
the grass will shed its moisture,
the fog will lift from the trees,
a new light will brighten the sky

and play in the drops
that hang on all things.
Your heart will beat out
a new gladness,
—if you let it happen.

Each day brings an hour of magic.
Listen to it!
Things will whisper their secrets.
You will know
what fills the herbs with goodness,
makes days change into nights,
turns the stars
and brings the change of seasons.
When you have come to know
some of nature's wise ways
beware of your complacency
for you cannot be wiser than nature.
You can only be as wise
as any man will ever hope to be,
—if you let it happen.

Our ways are good
but only in our world
If you like the flame
on the white man's wick
learn of his ways,
yet when you enter his world,
you will walk like a stranger
so you can bear his company.

For some time
bewilderment will,
like an ugly spirit
torment you.
Then rest on the holy earth
and wait for the good spirit.
He will return with new ways
as his gift to you,
—if you let it happen.

Use the heritage of silence
to observe others.
If greed has replaced the goodness
in a man's eyes
see yourself in him
so you will learn to understand
and preserve yourself.
Do not despise the weak,
it is compassion
that will make you strong.

Does not the rice
drop into your basket
whilst your breath
carries away the chaff?
There is good in everything,
—if you let it happen.

When the storms close in
and the eyes cannot find the horizon
you may lose much.
Stay with your love for life
for it is the very blood
running through your veins.
As you pass through the years
you will find much calmness
in your heart.
It is the gift of age,
and the colors of the fall
will be deep and rich,
—if you let it happen.

As I see beyond the days of now
I see a vision:
I see the faces of my people,
your sons' sons,
your daughters' daughters,
laughter fills the air
that is no longer yellow and heavy,
the machines have died,
quietness and beauty
have returned to the land.
The gentle ways of our race
have again put us
in the days of the old.
It is good to live!
It is good to die!
—This will happen.

23

Of all the teachings we receive
this one is the most important:

Nothing belongs to you
of what there is,

of what you take,
you must share.

Touch a child — they are my people.

The sunlight does not leave its marks
on the grass.
So we, too, pass silently.

The faces of the past are like leaves
that settle to the ground . . .

They make the earth rich and thick,
so that new fruit will come forth
every summer.

No longer
      can I give you a handful of berries as a gift,
no longer
      are the roots I dig used as medicine,
no longer
      can I sing a song to please the salmon,
no longer
      does the pipe I smoke make others sit
      with me in friendship,
no longer
      does anyone want to walk with me to the
      blue mountain to pray,
no longer
      does the deer trust my footsteps . . .

If you talk to animals they will talk with you
and you will know each other.

If you do not talk to them you will not know them,
and what you do not know you will fear.

What one fears one destroys.

O earth
for the strength
in my heart
I thank Thee.

O cloud
for the blood
in my body
I thank Thee.

O fire
for the shine
in my eyes
I thank Thee.

O sun
for the life
you gave to me
I thank Thee.

I am a native of North America.

In the course of my lifetime I have lived in two
distinct cultures. I was born into a culture that lived
in communal houses. My grandfather's house was
eighty feet long. It was called a smoke house, and
it stood down by the beach along the inlet. All my
grandfather's sons and their families lived in this
large dwelling. Their sleeping apartments were
separated by blankets made of bull rush reeds,
but one open fire in the middle served the cooking
needs of all. In houses like these, throughout the
tribe, people learned to live with one another;
learned to serve one another; learned to respect

the rights of one another. And children shared the thoughts of the adult world and found themselves surrounded by aunts and uncles and cousins who loved them and did not threaten them. My father was born in such a house and learned from infancy how to love people and be at home with them.

And beyond this acceptance of one another there was a deep respect for everything in nature that surrounded them. My father loved the earth and all it's creatures. The earth was his second mother. The earth and everything it contained was a gift from See-see-am . . . and the way to thank this great spirit was to use his gifts with respect.

I remember, as a little boy, fishing with him up Indian River and I can still see him as the sun rose above the mountain top in the early morning . . . I can see him standing by the water's edge with his arms raised above his head while he softly moaned . . . "Thank you, thank you". It left a deep impression on my young mind.

And I shall never forget his disappointment when once he caught me gaffing for fish "just for the fun of it". "My Son" he said, "The Great Spirit gave you those fish to be your brothers, to feed you when you are hungry. You must respect them. You must not kill them just for the fun of it."

This then was the culture I was born into and for some years the only one I really knew or tasted. This is why I find it hard to accept many of the things I see around me.

I see people living in smoke houses hundreds of times bigger than the one I knew. But the people in one apartment do not even know the people in the next and care less about them.

It is also difficult for me to understand the deep hate that exists among people. It is hard to understand a culture that justifies the killing of millions in past wars, and is at this very moment preparing bombs to kill even greater numbers. It is hard for me to understand a culture that spends more on wars and weapons to kill, than it does on education and welfare to help and develop.

It is hard for me to understand a culture that not only hates and fights his brothers but even attacks nature and abuses her. I see my white brothers going about blotting out nature from his cities. I see him strip the hills bare, leaving ugly wounds

on the face of mountains. I see him tearing things
from the bosom of mother earth as though she
were a monster, who refused to share her treasures
with him. I see him throw poison in the waters,
indifferent to the life he kills there; and he chokes
the air with deadly fumes.

My white brother does many things well for he is
more clever than my people but I wonder if he
knows how to love well. I wonder if he has ever
really learned to love at all. Perhaps he only loves
the things that are his own but never learned to love
the things that are outside and beyond him. And
this is, of course, not love at all, for man must love
all creation or he will love none of it. Man must

love fully or he will become the lowest of the animals. It is the power to love that makes him the greatest of them all . . . for he alone of all animals is capable of love.

Love is something you and I must have. We must have it because our spirit feeds upon it. We must have it because without it we become weak and faint. Without love our self esteem weakens. Without it our courage fails. Without love we can no longer look out confidently at the world. Instead we turn inwardly and begin to feed upon our own personalities and little by little we destroy ourselves.

You and I need the strength and joy that comes from knowing that we are loved. With it we are creative. With it we march tirelessly. With it, and with it alone, we are able to sacrifice for others.

There have been times when we all wanted so desperately to feel a re-assuring hand upon us . . . there have been lonely times when we so wanted a strong arm around us . . . I cannot tell you how deeply I miss my wife's presence when I return from a trip. Her love was my greatest joy, my strength, my greatest blessing.

I am afraid my culture has little to offer yours. But my culture did prize friendship and companionship. It did not look on privacy as a thing to be clung to, for privacy builds up walls and walls promote distrust. My culture lived in big family communities, and from infancy people learned to live with others.

My culture did not price the hoarding of private possessions, in fact, to hoard was a shameful thing to do among my people. The Indian looked on all

things in nature as belonging to him and he expected
to share them with others and to take only what
he needed.

Everyone likes to give as well as receive. No one
wishes only to receive all the time. We have taken
much from your culture . . . I wish you had taken
something from our culture . . . for there were some
beautiful and good things in it.

Soon it will be too late to know my culture, for
integration is upon us and soon we will have no
values but yours. Already many of our young people
have forgotten the old ways. And many have been
shamed of their Indian ways by scorn and ridicule.
My culture is like a wounded deer that has crawled
away into the forest to bleed and die alone.

The only thing that can truly help us is genuine
love. You must truly love us, be patient with us
and share with us. And we must love you — with
a genuine love that forgives and forgets . . . a love
that forgives the terrible sufferings your culture
brought ours when it swept over us like a wave
crashing along a beach . . . with a love that forgets
and lifts up its heads and sees in your eyes an
answering love of trust and acceptance.

This is brotherhood . . . anything less is not worthy
of the name.

I have spoken.

They say we do not show our feelings.
This is not so.

Everything is within,
where the heart pounds out the richness of our emotions.

The face only speaks
the language of the passing years.

Drive a car,
watch television,
and your fingers will find it difficult
to remember their skills.

Faster
the drum sounds
as the spirits move closer

the rattle shakes
and we dance.

47

48

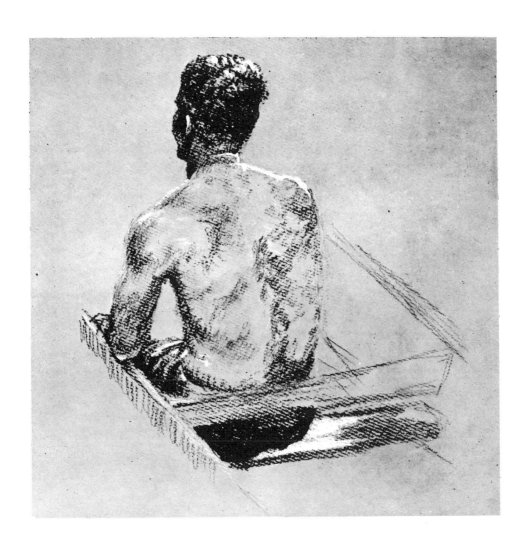

Many shores I have sailed to in my canoe,
often against strong winds.
Choose the tree well my brother,
if it is to carry you to distant shores.

When a man does
what needs to be done,
he does not know
the meaning of time.

I have sat many hours
on the steps outside my house,
and while I whittled
I tasted nature
and felt her throb of life.
Yet the strangers walking by
thought me lazy.

We all wander through life
united by the bond of creation
and become brothers
through gratitude.
We have much to be thankful for.
Let each of us
talk to the same Supreme Being
in his own way.

A man who cannot give thanks
for the food he eats
walks without the blessings of nature.

Once people knew how to live in harmony,
now the silence of nature
reaches few.

There are many who look,
but only some who see.

The earth is holy,
the feet that walk on it are blessed.

If the legends fall silent,
who will teach the children
of our ways?

When a man sits down in quietness
to listen to the teachings of his spirit
many things will come to him
in knowledge and understanding.
We have been so much luckier
because we never needed to communicate
in any other way than by thought or word.

This alone will no longer be possible.

We have diminished in numbers and paid
for our past with sorrow and pain
of which no generation of native people
is without its share.
We have suffered much,
now we stand to lose all
unless we preserve whatever is left
from the days of our ancestors.

To do this, the spoken word is not enough.

When a thought forms
it needs much time to grow.
Silence between spoken words
has always been the sign of deliberation.
In these new times of a modern world
where everything has become of value
silence has become time.
Time unused has become time wasted.
We are told: "Time is money."

It is harder to find somebody
who will listen, but everybody reads.
Therefore we must write about our ways,
our beliefs, our customs, our morals,
how we look at things and why,
how we lived, and how we live now.

To do this, we need the old and the young.

Soon there will be many books
that will tell of our ways
and perhaps will shame even those
who think us inferior
only because we are different.
To those who believe in the power
of the written word these books
will proclaim our cultural worth.
It has been done so for other races
and their teachings.
This is how our young people
will bring to you the true image
of our native people
and destroy the distortion
of which we have been the victims
for so long.
Then we will prosper in all things.
From our children will come those braves,
who will carry the torches to the places
where our ancestors rest.
There we will bow our heads
and chant the song of their honor.
This is how the void will be filled
between the old and the new ways.

The young and the old are closest to life.
They love every minute dearly.

If the very old will remember,
the very young will listen.

Keep a few embers
from the fire
that used to burn in your village,
some day go back
so all can gather again
and rekindle a new flame,
for a new life in a changed world.

Walk softly,
follow my footsteps
'til we meet at dawn.

Stand quietly,
let your lips give praise
to the new sun.

I have known you
when your forests were mine;
when they gave me my meat
and clothing.
I have known you
in your streams
and rivers
where your fish flashed
and danced in the sun,
where the waters said come,
come and eat of my abundance.
I have known you
in the freedom of your winds.
And my spirit,
like the winds,
once roamed your good lands.

For thousands of years
I have spoken the language of the land
and listened to its many voices.
I took what I needed
and found there was plenty for everyone.
The rivers were clear and thick with life,
the air was pure and gave way
to the thrashing of countless wings.
On land, a profusion of creatures abounded.
I walked tall and proud
knowing the resourcefulness of my people,

feeling the blessings of the Supreme Spirit.
I lived in the brotherhood of all beings.
I measured the day
by the sun's journey across the sky.
The passing of the year was told
by the return of the salmon
or the birds pairing off to nest.
Between the first campfire and the last
of each day I searched for food,
made shelter, clothing and weapons,
and always found time for prayer.

The wisdom and eloquence of my father
I passed on to my children,
so they too acquired faith,
courage, generosity, understanding,
and knowledge in the proper way of living.
Such are the memories of yesterday!
Today, harmony still lives in nature,
though we have less wilderness,
less variety of creatures.
Fewer people know the cougar's den
in the hills, nor have their eyes followed
the eagle's swoop, as he writes endless
circles into the warm air.

The wild beauty of the coastline
and the taste of sea fog remains hidden
behind the windows of passing cars.
When the last bear's skin has been taken
and the last ram's head has been mounted
and fitted with glass eyes,
we may find in them the reflection
of today's memories.
Take care, or soon our ears will strain
in vain to hear the creator's song.

When I pray,
I pray for all living things.
When I thank,
I thank for everything.

A man who lives and dies in the woods
knows the secret life of trees.

Look at the faces of my people:
You will find expressions of love and despair,
hope and joy, sadness and desire, and all the
human feelings that live in the hearts of people
of all colours. Yet, the heart never knows the
colour of the skin.

74

After the winter's cold and icy winds, life again flows up from the bosom of Mother Earth. And Mother Earth throws off dead stalks and withered limbs for they are useless. In their place new and strong saplings arise.

Already signs of new life are arising among my people after our sad winter has passed. We have discarded our broken arrows and our empty quivers, for we know what served us in the past can never serve us again.

Little things
are important,
because they are little
we see them
but do not understand them.

The beauty of the trees,
the softness of the air,
the fragrance of the grass,
        speaks to me.

The summit of the mountain,
the thunder of the sky,
the rhythm of the sea,
        speaks to me.

The faintness of the stars,
the freshness of the morning,
the dew drop on the flower,
        speaks to me.

The strength of fire,
the taste of salmon,
the trail of the sun,
And the life that never goes away,
        They speak to me.

And my heart soars.

84

My people's memory
reaches into the
beginning of all things.

A wild rose whispers sweetness to the squirrel,
a child loves everybody first.

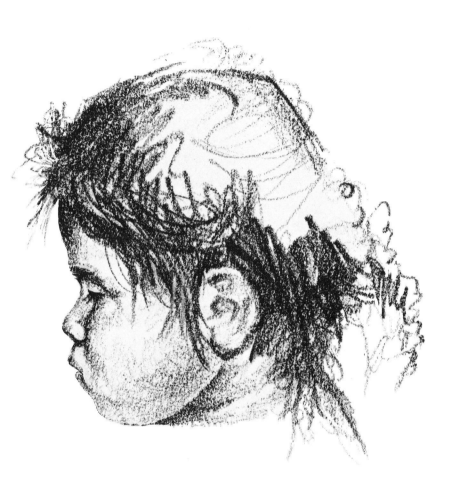

There is a longing in the heart of my people
to reach out and grasp that which is needed
for our survival. There is a longing among
the young of my nation to secure for them-
selves and their people the skills that will
provide them with a sense of worth and
purpose. They will be our new warriors.
Their training will be much longer and
more demanding than it was in olden days.
The long years of study will demand more
determination, separation from home and
family will demand endurance. But they
will emerge with their hand held forward,
not to receive welfare, but to grasp the
place in society that is rightly ours.

I am a chief, but my power to make war
is gone, and the only weapon left to me
is speech. It is only with tongue and speech
that I can fight my people's war.

Oh, Great Spirit! Give me back the courage
of the olden Chiefs. Let me wrestle with
my surroundings. Let me once again,
live in harmony with my environment.
Let me humbly accept this new culture
and through it rise up and go on. Like
the thunderbird of old, I shall rise again
out of the sea; I shall grab the instruments
of the white man's success — his
education, his skills. With these new tools
I shall build my race into the proudest
segment of your society. I shall see our
young braves and our chiefs sitting in
the houses of law and government, ruling
and being ruled by the knowledge and
freedoms of *our* great land.

93

This talk has been good!